Thou Harp of my Music

Thou Harp of my Music

Love Songs from the Gaelic

Collected and translated by
Alexander Carmichael

Selected and introduced by
C. J. Moore

Floris Books

The title is taken from
"Charm of grace" p.23

These verses are selected from the *Carmina Gadelica*
published in six volumes between 1900 and 1961.

This arrangement first published in 1999 by
Floris Books, 15 Harrison Gardens, Edinburgh
This arrangement © Floris Books, 1999

British Library CIP Data available

ISBN 0-86315-293-7

Printed in Great Britain
by Cromwell Press, Trowbridge, Wilts.

Contents

Introduction

The Gaelic oral tradition is unsurpassed for the light it sheds on the customs, folklore and beliefs of the Highlands and Islands crofting communities. For centuries, the hymns, songs and incantations, charms, prayers and rites of these "unlearned" people were handed down, preserved from generation to generation. Many of the sacred songs are believed to date from the foundation of Iona in the sixth century by Columba.

Almost all the daily activities of the people were accompanied by rituals or litanies in which old forms were given fresh and spontaneous utterance by the singer or storyteller. This freshness comes out nowhere more fully than in the love songs and love rites. Here we find not only the humour and vitality of dalliance and courtship but also, alongside love triumphant, the sadness and grief of love lost, love unrequited, love taken by disease or claimed by the seas — and perhaps most cruel of all, yet so commonplace through the troubled history of the clans, love a victim to enmity, betrayal and conflict.

Lovers met and courted in the social rituals of Michaelmas, set up home together, and toiled at fishing, at the loom and in the field, as long as health and life lasted. Their songs tell of delight and merriment in the feasts and gatherings of the year, as well as times of hardship, loss, fear and despair. Through all, their instinct was never far from a sense of beauty, and there is grace and nobility in the verses which utter even their most tragic experiences.

In the present selection, romantic love figures in all its moods — from courtship and marriage to grief and lamentation. But other aspects of love, as strongly felt in their own way, are represented, too. At one end we find pure story-telling, close to myth, in tales of courtly love and fairy lovers. At the other, we hear the warm and enduring voices of parents, of brothers and sisters, of friends, of the grateful or the admiring.

A good part of the voices are those of women. It is because the daily routine of the crofting communities brought women together for labours at which they could work with their hands, while chatting and singing the hours away in inventive compositions. This was a social forum in which feelings of all kinds towards men — jealousy, tenderness, annoyance, infatuation — could be expressed freely, often with wit and humour.

Then, of course, ever mingled with the human and familiar, there appears the sacred. What gives depth to the Celtic tradition is its awareness of spirituality, the sacred and the secular never separated, as we are told by Alexander Carmichael, the great nineteenth century gatherer of the oral literature. Perfect beauty resides in the holiness of Mary, Queen of Heaven, or her midwife and saint, Brigit, and the loveliness of a girl is a soul-gift, a grace bestowed from on high.

So in our opening section here, the love-story that is a life begins with the invocations of parents and relatives for the blessings and graces of beauty on the birth of a child.

Alexander Carmichael was a tax collector who travelled during a working lifetime throughout the Highlands and Islands. His deep affection for the customs and beliefs of the folk he met was accompanied by an acute sense of tragedy, as he watched the fading away of their oral literature — still kept among the older generation, but being rigorously suppressed as ignorant superstition by the social, educational and church pressures of his time.

Carmichael himself never doubted the special character of this cultural treasure being so carelessly discarded by the modern age:

> Whatever be the value of this work, it is genuine folklore, taken down from the lips of men and women, no part being copied from books. It is the product of faraway thinking, come down on the long stream of time. Who the thinkers and whence the stream, who can tell? Some of the hymns may have been composed within the cloistered cells of Derry and Iona, and some of the incantations among the cromlechs of Stonehenge and the standing-stones of Callarnis. These poems were composed by the learned, but they have not come down through the learned, but through the unlearned — not through the lettered few, but through the unlettered many — through the crofters and cottars, the herdsmen and shepherds, of the Highlands and Islands.

From the mouths of his own contributors, he heard painful stories of how the new age — in the form of

"ignorant school-teaching and clerical narrowness" —
despised the old:

> A young lady said: "When we came to Islay I was
> sent to the parish school to obtain a proper
> grounding in arithmetic. I was charmed with the
> schoolgirls and their Gaelic songs. But the
> schoolmaster — an alien like myself —
> denounced Gaelic speech and Gaelic songs. On
> getting out of school one evening the girls
> resumed a song they had been singing the previ-
> ous evening. I joined willingly, if timidly, my
> knowledge of Gaelic being small. The schoolmas-
> ter heard us, however, and called us back. He
> punished us till the blood trickled from our fin-
> gers, although we were big girls, with the dawn
> of womanhood upon us. The thought of that
> scene thrills me with indignation ..."

Many factors, Carmichael realized, had brought
about the decline of Gaelic literature:

> The Reformation, the Risings, the evictions, the
> Disruption, the schools and the spirit of the age.
> ... Ministers of Lewis used to say that the people
> of Lewis were little better than pagans till the
> Reformation.

It is true that the mind of the Celt was open to other
worlds — and not always those approved by Christian
theology. Love songs evoked brushes with fairy folk as
well as humans. Hunters who spent time in the hills,

young girls tending flocks alone or boys scouring lonely beaches for sea-weed or driftwood, were all vulnerable to the charm of fairy lovers. Tales of such were told as warnings.

Many were the incantations and rituals to guard against otherworldly dangers. For what should you say to protect yourself if you happened to meet a fairy in a lonely place? Words carried power in those communities. Powers of cursing and blessing, charms for good fortune or for protection against accident, illness or violence — invocations for all these were sewn into the daily pattern of work and play. To prosper meant guarding yourself against all the bad forces which wronged lovers and spiteful tongues could bring on your head.

So the words gathered here — tribute to the long painstaking work and passion of Alexander Carmichael — are not mere fictions and follies but the living expression of daily reality in the harsh but blessed environment of the islands. They express the very essence of Celtic lore: its liveliness, its lyrical response to the moment. Added to that, the intense challenging lifestyle from which these verses arose gives them their strength — a songful vigour and vitality which remind us of the awesome depth of power in the world from which we modern people have become separated.

C.J. Moore
February 1999

The Ceilidh

From Carmichael's Introduction to the *Carmina Gadelica*.

In a crofting community the people work in unison in the field during the day, and discuss together in the house at night. This meeting is called ceilidh — a word that throbs the heart of the Highlander wherever he be. The ceilidh is a literary entertainment where stories and tales, poems and ballads, are rehearsed and recited, and songs are sung, conundrums are put, proverbs are quoted, and many other literary matters are related and discussed. This institution is admirably adapted to cultivate the heads and to warm the hearts of an intelligent, generous people. Let me briefly describe the ceilidh as I have seen it.

In a crofting townland there are several story-tellers who recite the oral literature of their predecessors. The story-tellers of the Highlands are as varied in their subjects as are literary men and women elsewhere. One is a historian narrating events simply and concisely; another is a historian with a bias, colouring his narrative according to his leanings. One is an inventor, building fiction upon fact, mingling his materials, and investing the whole with the charm of novelty and the halo of romance. Another is a reciter of heroic poems and ballads, bringing the different characters before the mind as clearly as the sculptor brings the figure before the eye. One gives the songs of the chief poets, with interesting accounts of their authors, while another, generally a woman, sings, to weird airs, beautiful old songs, some of them Arthurian. There are various other narrators, singers, and speakers, but I have never heard aught that should not be said nor sung.

The romance school has the largest following, and I go there, joining others on the way. The house of the story-teller is already full, and it is difficult to get inside and away from the cold wind and soft sleet without. But with that politeness native to the people, the stranger is pressed to come forward and occupy the seat vacated for him beside the houseman. The house is roomy and clean, if homely, with its bright peat fire in the middle of the floor. There are many present — men and women, boys and girls. All the women are seated, and most of the men. Girls are crouched between the knees of fathers or brothers or friends, while boys are perched wherever — boy-like — they can climb. The houseman is twisting twigs of heather into ropes to hold down thatch, a neighbour crofter is twining quicken roots into cords to tie cows, while another is plaiting bent grass into baskets to hold meal.

The housewife is spinning, a daughter is carding, another daughter is teazing, while a third daughter, supposed to be working, is away in the background conversing in low whispers with the son of a neighbouring crofter. Neighbour wives and neighbour daughters are knitting, sewing, or embroidering. The conversation is general: the local news, the weather, the price of cattle, these leading up to higher themes — the clearing of the glens (a sore subject), the war, the parliament, the effects of the sun upon the earth and the moon upon the tides. The speaker is eagerly listened to and is urged to tell more. But he pleads that he came to hear and not to speak.

The stranger asks the houseman to tell a story, and after a pause the man complies. The tale is full of incident, action, and pathos. It is told simply yet graphically, and at times dramatically — compelling the undivided attention of the listener. At the pathetic scenes and distressful events the bosoms of the women may be seen to heave and their silent tears to fall. Truth overcomes craft, skill conquers strength, and bravery is rewarded. Occasionally a momentary excitement occurs when heat and sleep overpower a boy and he tumbles down among the people below, to be trounced out and sent home. When the story is ended it is discussed and commented upon, and the different characters praised or blamed according to their merits and the views of the critics.

Alexander Carmichael
Edinburgh 1899

Blessings, graces
and charms

For the Celtic people, St Bride was the greatest protectress of all, and her feast-day on February 1st, one of the most important in the annual calendar. Carmichael writes:

> ... there were several Brides, Christian and pre-Christian, whose personalities have become confused in the course of centuries — the attributes of all being now popularly ascribed to one. Bride is said to preside over fire, over art, over all beauty, *fo cheabhar agus fo chuan* (beneath the sky and beneath the sea). And man being the highest type of ideal beauty, Bride presides at his birth and dedicates him to the Trinity. She is the Mary and the Juno of the Gael. She is much spoken of in connection with Mary, generally in relation to the birth of Christ. She was the aid-woman of the Mother of Nazareth in the lowly stable, and she is the aid-woman of the mothers of Uist in their humble homes.

Bride, or Brigit, was therefore invoked at the birth of a child not only for physical succour but also for the spiritual wellbeing of the infant:

> When a woman is in labour, the midwife or the woman next her in importance goes to the door of the house, and standing on the doorstep, with her hands on the jambs, softly beseeches Bride to come.

The saint's blessings and graces would follow a girl all her life, into womanhood and wifehood, and if her household fell upon difficult times, it would be because Bride was offended and had withdrawn her presence. The seasonal *rituals and prayers that kept Bride's protection for a home were therefore considered vitally important.*

In a mysterious interweaving of the pagan and Biblical traditions, a particular feature of Bride's feast-day was the attention paid to the serpent. This could take the form of ritual propitiation —"I will not molest the serpent, nor will the serpent molest me" — or the widespread Bride's day custom of the woman "pounding the serpent" in effigy, echoing God's words in Genesis:

> *I will put enmity between you and the woman*
> *and between your seed and her seed;*
> *he shall bruise your head*
> *and you shall bruise his heel. (RSV 3:15)*

Womanhood of Brigit or Praises of Brigit

Brigit daughter of Dugall the Brown
Son of Aodh son of Art son of Conn
Son of Criara son of Cairbre son of Cas
Son of Cormac son of Cartach son of Conn.

Brigit of the mantles,
Brigit of the peat-heap,
Brigit of the twining hair,
Brigit of the augury.

Brigit of the white feet,
Brigit of calmness,
Brigit of the white palms,
Brigit of the kine.

Brigit, woman-comrade,
Brigit of the peat-heap,
Brigit, woman-helper,
Brigit, woman mild.

Brigit, own tress of Mary,
Brigit, Nurse of Christ —
Each day and each night
That I say the Descent of Brigit,

I shall not be slain,
I shall not be wounded,
I shall not be put in cell,
I shall not be gashed,
I shall not be torn in sunder,

I shall not be despoiled,
I shall not be down-trodden,
I shall not be made naked,
I shall not be rent,
Nor will Christ
Leave me forgotten.

Nor sun shall burn me,
Nor fire shall burn me,
Nor beam shall burn me,
Nor moon shall burn me.

Nor river shall drown me,
Nor brine shall drown me,
Nor flood shall drown me,
Nor water shall drown me.

Nightmare shall not lie on me,
Black-sleep shall not lie on me,
Spell-sleep shall not lie on me,
Luaths-luis shall not lie on me.

I am under the keeping
Of my Saint Mary;
My companion beloved
Is Brigit.

Blessing of Brigit

I am under the shielding
   Of good Brigit each day;
I am under the shielding
   Of good Brigit each night.

I am under the keeping
   Of the Nurse of Mary,
Each early and late,
   Every dark, every light.

Brigit is my comrade-woman,
   Brigit is my maker of song,
Brigit is my helping-woman,
   My choicest of women, my guide.

Charm of grace

The charm placed by Brigit,
Maiden of graces,
On the white daughter of the king,
Gile-Mhin the beauteous.

The form of God is behind thee,
The form of Christ is before thee,
The stream of Spirit is through thee,
To succour and aid thee.

The bloom of God is upon thee,
The bloom of Christ is upon thee,
The bloom of Spirit is upon thee,
To bathe thee and make thee fair.

Grace is upwards over thee,
Grace is downwards over thee,
Grace of graces without gainsaying,
Grace of Father and of Lord.

Excellence of men,
Excellence of women,
Excellence of council,
Excellence of lover,
Excellence of sons and of daughters.

Excellence of dells,
Excellence of knolls,
Excellence of hollows,

Excellence of hills,
Excellence of horses and of heroes.

Excellence of travel,
Excellence of journey,
Excellence of small town,
Excellence of great town,
Excellence of sea and of shore.

Excellence of beauty,
Excellence of radiance,
Excellence of goodness,
Excellence of heaven,
Excellence of day and of night.

Excellence of form,
Excellence of voice,
Excellence of complexion,
Excellence of cattle,
Excellence of curd and of butter.

Thou art the star of each night,
Thou art the brightness of each morn,
Thou art the tidings of each guest,
Thou art the enquiry of every land.

Thou shalt travel a rough ground
And thou shalt not redden thy foot:
Jesus is guarding thee,
Jesus is by thy hand.

The crown of the King is around thy head,
The diadem of the Son is around thy brow,
The might of the Spirit is in thy breast:
Thou shalt go forth and come homeward safe.

Thou shalt journey upward
And come again down,
Thou shalt journey over ocean
And come again hither;

No peril shall befall thee
On knoll nor on bank,
In hollow nor in meadow,
On mount nor in glen.

The shield of Michael is over thee,
King of the bright angels,
To shield thee and to guard thee
From thy summit to thy sole.

Nor shall man
Nor shall woman
Nor shall son
Nor shall daughter

Make glance nor wish,
Hate nor jealousy,
Love nor eye,
Envy nor durance

That shall sunder thee,
That shall lie upon thee,
That shall subdue thee,
That shall wound thee.

Host shall not make,
False one shall not make,
Fairy shall not make,
World shall not make

Sling nor catapult,
Spear nor shaft,
Axe nor javelin,
Hook nor sword,

That shall affect thee,
That shall afflict thee,
That shall wound thee,
That shall overpower thee.

No smith shall make,
No craftsman shall make,
No mason shall make,
No wright shall make

Gear nor tool,
Weapon nor device,
Tackle nor instrument,
Frame nor invention,

Of copper nor stone,
Of brass nor iron,

Of wood nor bronze,
Of gold nor silver,

That shall check thee,
That shall enclose thee,
That shall rend thee,
That shall bridle thee,
Thither nor hither,
Earth nor land,
Here nor yonder,
Down nor up,
Above nor below,
Sea nor shore,
In the sky aloft,
In the deep beneath.

Thou nut of my heart,
Thou face of my sun,
Thou harp of my music,
Thou crown of my sense;

Thou art the love of the God of Life,
Thou art the love of tender Christ,
Thou art the love of Spirit Holy,
Thou art the love of each living creature,
Thou art the love of each living creature.

Charm for the face of a maiden

The beauty of God is in thy face,
The Son of God is protecting thee
From the wicked ones of the world,
The King of the stars is before thee.

The beauty of Mary of the deep love,
A tongue mannerly, mild, modest,
Fair hair between thy two eyebrows —
Fionn son of Cumhall between these.*

Since it is Mary and Jesus her Son
Who set this pleasantness in thy face,
May the taste of mild honey be upon thee
And upon every word thou speakest,

To simple and to noble,
To men and to tender women,
From this day that we have here
Till the day of the ending of thy life,
In reliance on the beloved and the powers
        eternal,
In reliance on the God of life and the shielding of
        His Son.

* *Fionn* means "fair."

Courtship and Marriage

The traditional season for courtship was Michaelmas when the crofting communities came together to honour one of the most important saints in their calendar — St Michael, patron of the sea and sailors, and of horses and horsemen.

Ceremonies on this occasion were rich and varied and many days were spent in preparation, including the baking of the Michael cakes to be eaten with friends. Riding around, "circuiting," the burial-grounds was one ritual during which the young could meet and socialise. Both men and women showed off their prowess at riding in the races that followed. The day culminated in dancing and merry-making which went on all night. Carmichael writes:

> At the circuiting by day and at the ball at night, youths and maidens exchange simple gifts in token of good feeling. The girls give the men bonnets, hose, garters, cravats, purses, plaids, and other things of their own making, and the men give the girls brooches of silver, brass, bronze, or copper, knives, scissors, snoods, combs, mirrors, and various other things.
>
> On the Sunday afternoon before St Michael's feast-day, the women go into the fields and hillsides to find carrots. These are washed and bound, to be given as tokens of prosperity and fertility. The women sing as they work, and celebrate loudly if they find a forked carrot which is a sign of special blessing.

At other times, too, while working, especially at cloth-making in the home, the women sang together. Sung among women alone, these songs were often frank commentaries on the men in their lives:

During the work the women sing lively, stirring, emphatic songs. One sings a verse, all join in the chorus. The leader usually sits at the head of the waulking-frame; if she is advanced in life she is not allowed to work, in which case she sits a few feet back and in a line with the frame. The women keep time with their arms or feet.

Most of the songs sung are war-songs, love-songs, boating-songs, and hunting-songs. In all these the lovers or husbands or chiefs of the women form the subject of the song, which is fervid and personal to a degree. There are also perhaps impromptus, on some local topic, perhaps on the real or supposed love-affairs of one or more of the girls present.

Generally the waulking-women are young maidens, a few married women of good voice being distributed among them. They sing as they work, one singing the song, the others the chorus. Their songs are varied, lively, and adapted to the class of work. Most of them are love-songs, with an occasional impromptu song on some passing event — perhaps on the casual stranger who has looked in, perhaps a wit combat between two of the girls about the real or supposed merits or demerits of their respective lovers. These wit combats are much enjoyed, being often clever, caustic, and apt.

The apple tree

O apple tree,
Apple branch,
Apple tree,
Tree of apples.

When thou goest to the wood to strip it,
Recognise the tree which is mine there,
The tree of softest, sweetest apples,
The branching pear-like tree full of apples,
Its roots growing and its top bending.

I have a tree in the Green Rock,
Another tree hard by the garden gate;
If Mackay were but here,
Or the redoubtable Neil, his brother,
My dower would not go unpaid,
With milch kine and heifers in calf,
With sheep black-faced and white,
And with geldings for the ploughing.

A versatile man is Mackay,
He can make silk of May wool,
And satin of heather if need were;
He can make wine of mountain water.
An ingenious man is Mackay,
He can dry grain without fuel,
It is with his fists he bruises it.

Mackay of the gusseted coat
Would not require heavy armour;

Rider of the chestnut horses,
He would put golden shoes on their hooves,
Traverser of the broken ground.

My dear, my love is the valiant youth,
I would go with thee through the branchy wood,
I would fashion and sew thy shirt
With slender needle and pure-white thread;
I would wash it thereafter
On slippery slab in the bright river;
I would dry it on the tips of the branches,
I would place it folded in thy page's hand.

O apple tree, may God be with thee,
May the moon and the sun be with thee,
May the east and west winds be with thee,
May everything that ever was be with thee.

The promises

My lover gave to me a knife
That would cut the sapling withe,
That would cut the soft and hard,
Long live the hand that gave.

My lover promised me a snood,*
Ay, and a brooch and comb,
And I promised, by the wood,
To meet him at rise of sun.

My lover promised me a mirror
That my beauty I might see,
Yes, and a coif and ring,
And a dulcet harp of chords.

He vowed me those and a fold of kine,
And a palfrey of the steeds,
And a barge, pinnacled white,
That would safely cross the seas.

A thousand blessings, a thousand victories
To my lover who left me yestreen,
He gave to me the promise lasting,
Be his Shepherd God's own Son.

---

* *Snood*. Headwear of a married woman.

A missing knife

I lost the beautiful knife
  On Sunday just past,

It was no longer than a needle
  And it was better than a sword.

It fell among the rushes
  And I have not found it yet;

I am tired searching for it
  At the foot of the slope.

I would not give it on loan
  To mother or father,

Or to Angus MacDiarmid —
  Were he to ask, he would not get it.

Love Charm

It is not love knowledge to thee
To draw water through a reed,
But the love of him [her] thou choosest,
With his [her] warmth to draw to thee.

Arise thou early on the day of the Lord,
To the broad flat flag,
Take with thee the foxglove
And the butterbur.

Lift them on thy shoulder
In a wooden shovel,
Get thee nine stems of ferns
Cut with an axe,

The three bones of an old man,
That have been drawn from the grave,
Burn them on a fire of faggots,
And make them all into ashes.

Shake it in the very breast of thy lover,
Against the sting of the north wind,
And I will pledge, and warrant thee,
That man [woman] will never leave thee.

Waulking song

My love is to thee, son of the laird of Sórasdal!
I hate the man who has cast thee down,
And against him who destroyed his country
That will yet come to be reckoned,
The Campbells will be driven out,
And the rabble of the sowens scattered.

Sad that I and my chosen love
Were not in yonder wood arising;
Well would I wash thy shirt,
I would dry it on the tips of the boughs,
I would set it clean in thy page's hand.

Sad that I and the splendid youth
Were not on the summit of the sharp steep peaks,
With no living man beholding us.
In good repute we would come home,
The red snood would be folded by,
The peaked kertch would come into fashion.*

* *Snood/kertch:* The change of headwear from maidenhood to
   marriage.

St Kilda waulking song

I would make the fair cloth for thee,
Thread as the thatch-rope stout.

I would make the feathered buskin for thee,
Thou beloved and importunate of men.

I would give thee the precious anchor,
And the family gear which my grandfather
    had.

My love is the hunter of the bird,
Who earliest comes over misty sea.

My love the sailor of the waves,
Great the cheer his brow will show.

Circuiting song

Carmichael writes: "The circuiting song is sung by the maidens around the waulking frame, the matrons taking no part beyond an occasional lift with the chorus. As the song goes round every maiden present has an opportunity of trying her talent at impromptu verse. In these verses the girls banter one another about their lovers or supposed lovers, their merits and demerits, mental and physical endowments, virtues and defects of any kind coming in for special attention. Some of these impromptus are clever and amusing, and some occasionally bitter."

The following song, full of bitterness, was sung by a girl whose lover left her for a young woman of greater wealth.

> Last night I got not a wink of sleep,
> Hill! hill! hó! hillin ó!
> This night I shall not get as much,
> Hill! hill! hó! hillin ó!
>
> Though she were tattered and brindled,
> Her dusky cattle will fetch her out.
>
> Though she were tattered and shaggy,
> Fat and fair are her father's cattle.
>
> Though she were wizened and shrivelled,
> Fair and white are her horned cattle.
>
> Though she were hungry and like death,
> Oh my love the hidden windfall!

Though her eyes were watery, hollow,
And her mouth like amber, she'll get a lover.

But I lie snug, easy and sleepful,
Without cattle black or red or dappled.

Last night I got not a wink of sleep,
Hill! hill! hó! hillin ó!
This night I shall not get as much,
Hill! hill! hó! hillin ó!

Postcard

Floris Books
15 Harrison Gardens
Edinburgh
EH11 1SH
Great Britain

If you are interested in other publications from Floris Books, please return this card with your name and address.

Name _____
                                Surname

Address _____

_____

_____
                                Postcode

I am interested in following subjects:

☐C Celtic

☐R Religion

☐S Science

☐H Health & parenting

☐J Children's books

☐A Crafts & activities

☐ Please send me your catalogue once

☐ Please send me your catalogue regularly

I found this card in: _____
                                Book title

PC-95.05

Verse at the waulking frame

Thou girl over there, may the sun be against thee!
Thou hast taken from me my autumn carrot,
My Michaelmas carrot from my pillow,
My procreant buck among the goats.

But if thou hast, it was not without help,
But with the black cunning of the dun women;
Thou art the little she-goat that lifted the bleaching,
I am the little gentle cow that gave no milking.

Stone in shoe be thy bed for thee,
Husk in tooth be thy sleep for thee,
Prickle in eye be thy life for thee,
Restless watching by night and by day.

St Kilda lilt

HE: Away bent spade, away straight spade,
  Away each goat and sheep and lamb;
  Up my rope, up my snare —
  I have heard the gannet upon the sea!

  Thanks to the Being, the gannets are come,
  Yes, and the big birds along with them;
  Dark dusky maid, a cow in the fold!
  A brown cow, a brown cow, a brown cow beloved,
  A brown cow, my dear one, that would milk
   the milk for thee,
  Ho ro ru ra ree, playful maid,
  Dark dusky maid, a cow in the fold!
  The birds are a-coming, I hear their tune!

SHE: Truly my sweetheart is the herdsman
  Who would threaten the staff and would not strike!
  Dark dusky maid, a cow in the fold!
  The birds are a-coming, I hear their tune!

HE: Mary, my dear love is the maid,
  Though dark her locks her body is fragrant!
  Dark dusky maid, a cow in the fold!
  The birds are a-coming, I hear their tune!

SHE: Thou art my handsome joy, thou art my sweetheart,
  Thou gavest me first the honied fulmar!
  Dark dusky maid, a cow in the fold!
  The birds are a-coming, I hear their tune!

HE: Thou art my turtle-dove, thou art my mavis,
    Thou art my melodious harp in the sweet morning.
    Dark dusky maid, a cow in the fold!
    The birds are a-coming, I hear their tune!

SHE: Thou art my treasure, my lovely one, my huntsman,
    Yesterday thou gavest me the gannet and the auk.
    Dark dusky maid, a cow in the fold!
    The birds are a-coming, I hear their tune!

HE: I gave thee love when thou wast but a child,
    Love that shall not wane till I go beneath the earth.
    Dark dusky maid, a cow in the fold!
    The birds are a-coming, I hear their tune!

SHE: Thou art my hero, thou art my basking sunfish,
    Thou gavest me the puffin and the black-headed
        guillemot.
    Dark dusky maid, a cow in the fold!
    The birds are a-coming, I hear their tune!

HE:The mirth of my eyes and the essence of my joy
        thou art,
    And my sweet-sounding lyre in the mountain of mist.
    Dark dusky maid, a cow in the fold!
    The birds are a-coming, I hear their tune!

SHE:May the Being keep thee, the Creator aid thee,
    The Holy Spirit be behind thy rope!
    Dark dusky maid, a cow in the fold!
    A brown cow, a brown cow, a brown cow beloved,

A brown cow, my dear one, that would milk the
    milk for thee,
Ho ro ru ra ree, playful maid,
Dark dusky maid, a cow in the fold!

There is music in the marriage house

This verse was uttered by a maiden whose lover had forsaken her and was arranging, with the usual feast and merrymaking, a marriage with another girl in the townland.

The words were repeated to the errant lover, and he said: "That is true, thou best beloved!" and took up his plaid, staff and bonnet and returned whence he had come.

There is music in the marriage house,
There is ale, there is speaking;
But were there remembrance of the good that was,
'Tis the good that was which would be.

The vixen

Catherine's the wench
    Perverse and uncivil,
Unloveable, not plump,
    Graceless and dour;
'Tis my prayer each morning
To the court of the angels
That I be shielded from the hussy
    Headstrong and hard,
That she be not healthy
    Nor long-lived nor lasting!

'Tis my prayer each evening
Both Sunday and weekday
That the she-fool be stowed
    With the rabble of the graves;
Shortened be the life
Of herself and her people,
Her goats and her sheep,
    Her stock and her kine:
Be they stolen and plundered,
    Be they blasted and burned!

On her sheep be disease
Virulent, filthy,
With scab and with maggot,
    Rot and bloody flux,
Be they wasted by venom,
Be they sundered by dogs,
By honey-hound, by fierce wolf,
    By russet fox!

'Tis my prayer each hour
To the Crown of grace
That Catherine and her cows
   Be hapless and wan,
That she have no daughter nor son,
Her cows no calf nor milk,
No fatness and no cheer,
   No comely look nor beauty,
But be each night and day
   Sulky and glum.

Be her summer short,
   Surly and grim,
Her winter long,
   Flaying with cold,
Her spring snowy,
   Shrivelled, hard,
Her autumn ice-sheeted,
   Grievous, sullen,
Storm-harassed, disastrous,
   Calamitous, evil,
Sharpening outward,
Shortening inward,
Dearth to southward,
   Dearth to northward,
Dearth eastward and westward
   I ask be hers eternally!

Dearth from below be hers,
   Dearth from above,
Dearth from on high be hers,
   Dearth from beneath,

Dearth be east of her,
　Dearth be west,
Dearth be south of her,
　Dearth be north,
The dearth of the seven
　Miserable dearths
For ever and for ever
　I ask be hers eternally!

I pray to Peter,
　I pray to Paul,
I pray to James,
　I pray to John,
To John the Baptist,
　To Luke the Physician,
And to every saint
　And apostle that has followed them,
To kindly Columba
　And saintly Patrick,
To Mary mild
　And Brigit beloved,
To Ariel resplendent
　And to Michael of the blades,
To the Light of peace
　And to the Seer of the hills,
To guard and to keep me,
　On sea and on land,
From the vixenish wench
　In yonder town,
The vixenish wench
　In yonder town!

The brave men

The brave men are
On the flat of the moor,
And the beautiful women
On the flat of the glen,
With their grey plaids
And their pure-white feet,
And though sweet is the flesh
It is venison I sought.

My love are the households
On whom gloom would not settle,
Who would procure venison
Where lead would not reach the birds,
And who would not require powder
To wake them into activity,
The killers of the solan goose —
Much fair fame is theirs to tell of.

But a man of Clan Farquhar,
I would not leave thee neglected in a corner,
Seeing I am so persuaded
That thy conduct is faultless;

Thou wouldst bring the razorbill
From the ledges of the Dunan,
And didst thou but get practice
Thou wouldst harry the fulmar.

And a man of Clan Donald,
'Twere not right to rebuff him;

Thou art fashioned like a bull,
Thick of neck and broad of shoulder;
If I be not mistaken
Thou art the mightiest of thy clan —
Stouter the calf of thy leg
Than a well-matured body!

Giùran

Giùran son of Giùran is
    The unsheather of swords,
The ranger of the countryside
    And the scourge of black Saxons;
And despite all the resentment,
    The gossip and talk,
Giùran son of Giùran is
    My love of them all.

I spent a year in delirium
    Awaiting thy love;
I spent a year in a fever,
    My word! I had cause;
My mother was wrangling,
    My father was enraged,
But Giùran of heroic deeds
    Is the dearest in the world to me.

I spent more than a year
    In the fever of thy love;
I spent more than a year,
    My word! 'twas not a trifle;
My father was cursing,
    My mother was weeping,
But Giùran of the hostages
    Is my darling of men.

Sain mine own lover in the field

Thou youth who goest in the chase,
There was a time when I was thy chosen one,
The maiden now pillowed by thy face,
Once methought she was not thy choice.

Thou man the most comely who moves on plain,
Much noble blood is kin to thee;
O Thou who wast crucified above the others,
Sain mine own lover in the field!

A sprightly fellow is the stag
In the brindled bower dwelling,
Yet though strong and sturdy be his bound,
He cannot aye escape from death.

My loved one is beauteous and fair-shapen,
A hand of valour which a blade well becomes,
A man welcoming, mild, generous, liberal,
Blithe, mannerly, pleasant of temper, well-endowed.

Love and sadness

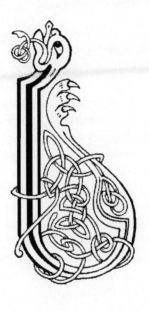

The precarious livelihood of the crofters forced them to face danger every day as they fished in the difficult currents and winds around the islands. Equally, while rescuing livestock among the rocks and bogs of the hills, or at hunting or gathering seabirds' eggs on the cliffs, a sudden slip could bring tragedy and the loss of a husband or lover, perhaps not to be seen again.

Added to natural hazards were the perils of war and feuding between clan families. The story attached to the haunting "Lullaby in the Snow" sets the mood:

> The night after the massacre of Glen Coe officers and soldiers were out searching the hills and dales for any stray fugitives who might have escaped the massacre. Hearing the sound of the pipes, they followed it, thinking that this might be some MacDonald guiding his friends to safety. Eager to wreak their vengeance on the clan they hated, they followed the piping through mud and mire, swamp and stream, snow wreath and rock cleft, till they reached a distant tarn among the high mountains. Here the music sank down in the depths of the tarn and died softly away as dies the eerie sough of the western wind.
>
> The people maintain that the piper was one of the good fairies of the mound.
>
> Beaten and battered by the storm, with baffled rage in their hearts and curses on their lips, the soldiers returned. They heard upon the wind the screaming of a child. The officer in command called out to the nearest soldier: "Go and put a twist in the neck of that brat."

As the man neared the place from which the screams were coming, he heard the one most beautiful music that ever ear heard, music more beautiful than the lip of the fairy women in the knoll. Who was this but a young mother who had escaped the massacre, lulling her child to sleep the sleep of death amid the snow?

The soldier remembered her whom he had left at home beside the fire with a little beautiful beloved babe upon her breast, singing a quiet croon of sleep to him, and the blood of Clan Donald in the veins of both. And it chanced that the gentle croon of music that the child's mother was singing in the snow was the very same music as he had last heard when he left his kin and his home many a day and year before that. The soldier wrapped the woman and her child in his plaid, gave them what food and drink he had, and left them to overtake his comrades. On the way he came upon a wolf devouring the body of a woman who had escaped alive from the scene of the massacre. He slew the wolf and showed the officer the blood upon his sword. By the mercy of God and through the soldier's compassion mother and child survived. Descendants of the child are still living, and the tradition is current and believed throughout the districts of Appin and Lochaber.

The lullaby of the snow

Cold, cold this night is my bed,
   Cold, cold this night is my child,
Lasting, lasting this night thy sleep,
   I in my shroud and thou in mine arm.

Over me creeps the shadow of death,
   The warm pulse of my love will not stir,
The wind of the heights thy sleep-lulling,
   The close-clinging snow of the peaks thy mantle.

Over thee creeps the hue of death,
   White angels are floating in the air,
The Son of grace each season guards thee,
The Son of my God keeps the watch with me.

Though loud my cry my plaint is idle,
   Though sore my struggle no friend shares it;
Thy body-shirt is the snow of the peaks,
   Thy death-bed the fen of the valleys.

Thine eye is closed, thy sleep is heavy,
   Thy mouth to my breast, but thou seekest no milk;
My croon of love thou shalt never know,
   My plaint of love thou shalt never tell.

A cold arm-burden my love on my bosom,
   A frozen arm-burden without life or breath;
May the angels of God make smooth the road,
   May the angels of God be calling us home.

A hard frost no thaw shall subdue,
   The frost of the grave which no spring shall
      make green,
A lasting sleep which morn shall not break,
   The death-slumber of mother and child.

Heavenly light directs my feet,
   The music of the skies gives peace to my soul,
Alone I am under the wing of the Rock,
   Angels of God calling me home.

Cold, cold, cold is my child,
   Cold, cold is the mother who watches thee,
Sad, sad, sad is my plaint,
   As the tinge of death creeps over me.

O Cross of the heavens, sign my soul,
   O Mother of breastlings, shield my child,
O Son of tears whom a mother nurtured,
   Show Thy tenderness in death to the needy.

Rowing song of the oaken galley

My treasure among the men of the sun,
I have seen thee not today nor yesterday.
I have seen no man thy like,
Except thou come, O John son of James,
In thy youth before death has struck thee.
Thou wast the grandson of Roderick the generous,
And great-grandson of Torquil of the keen blades,
Seed of the woman who won esteem;
Thou hast left my spirit grieving and tearful.
'S na hada hia hi 's na hi ho hua.

My treasure among the men of the oar-banks,
When thou wouldst go to thy boat
That was the work that well became thee,
Thy lads would be in the oar-bank,
Thyself wouldst be at thy boat's helm,
A champion-like, valiant, powerful man.
'S na hada hia hi 's na hi ho hua.

My treasure and my ransom and my dower is
Young John, son of James, of the full round eyes,
Blue is thine eye, and it is no mockery,
Yesterday thou didst sail through the Sound of Harris,
And my own good wish to thee for thy safe coming.
'S na hada hia hi 's na hi ho hua.

My treasure among the men of the mountain,
When thou wouldst go to the peaks
Truly thy lodging would not be empty,
But with slender-muzzled gun

Or with the knobbed bow of yew,
Breaking bones wherever it struck,
Welcoming ever him of the belling.
    'S na hada hia hi 's na hi ho hua.

My treasure among the men of the sea,
I saw thee passing downward by;
Mayest thou enjoy the tressed maiden of the snood,
Daughter of the lord of Glen Shee,
Of kindred widespread and many,
A bright form from the vine-slope art thou,
Thou shalt get a fold of jet-black cattle.
    'S na hada hia hi 's na hi ho hua.

My treasure among the men of deftness,
When thou wouldst turn to sailing
She would catch the breeze between the sheets,
The creak of the oars was music for thee,
Rudder behind her and a valiant, skilful man
Steering her in her proper course.
    'S na hada hia hi 's na hi ho hua.

My treasure and my ransom and my hoard
Are the men of the black and brown locks
Who would pound the ocean,
Who would souse her oaken timbers,
Who would drink red wine in waves
And who would carry off a spoil.
    'S na hada hia hi 's na hi ho hua.

My treasure and my ransom and my dower,
When thou wouldst go to sea

59

Truly thy hand was not found feeble
Though thou wast but a child;
Wooden pins would be twisted from her oaken planks,
She would shed the rove from every rivet's head;
Thy craft was not decayed,
And thy sailing was not inshore.
  'S na hada hia hi 's na hi ho hua.

My treasure and my ransom and my hoard,
Beauty of head grew richly on thee,
Hair in luxuriant precious locks
Well combed, of goodly cut;
And were I a bard I would make an oar-song,
And were I a carpenter I would make ships,
And here behind thee I needs must abide.

Late it was I saw yestreen

Late it was I saw yestreen
    A red-robed man upon the glen;
My heart rejoiced at his step,
    Methought it was thyself I saw.

Methought it was thyself I saw,
    Hunter of venison of the dun deer,
Traveller of the heaths and hills,
    Hunter of a thousand mighty stags.

Hunter of a thousand mighty stags,
    May gentle Brigit be close to thee,
May gentle Mary guard thy body,
    Fair white Michael guard thy head.

Sleep has forsaken me

Sleep has forsaken me since Shrovetide,
    Often I turn
In hope to see thy speeding ship
    On black-blue ocean.

Surpassing swift thy bark grey-timbered
    From the slope of Lochlann,
Each plank of her smooth as the swans' plumage
    On a loch's billows.

Of Alba's three prime warriors one far faring,
    This grieves me sore,
Far afield without folk or dwelling
    In the Isle of Man.

Would, Oh King! that thy grief's burden
    Were spread in thy land,
Upon each man his share, and on me
    Full share of three!

Love of youths art thou on a morning early
    In van of battle,
Love of women in mirth of evening
    When harp is playing.

This I would ask, a blade in thy right hand
    In a narrow pass,
There encountering them who hate thee,
    Blood blinding them.

There would come the carrion-crow and raven
   At the dawn's breaking,
Would drink their fill from the pools
   Brimming, blood-red.

Little bird

Little bird! O little bird!
I wonder at what thou doest,
Thou singing merry far from me,
I in sadness all alone!

Little bird! O little bird!
I wonder at how thou art,
Thou high on the tips of branching boughs,
I on the ground a-creeping!

Little bird! O little bird!
Thou art music far away,
Like the tender croon of the mother loved
In the kindly sleep of death.

Thou speckled troutling

"In the holy wells of the Isles there lived, through genera-tions, a trout which in the thoughts of the folk was account-ed pious as a monk and worldly — wise as a druid. To such a trout went the maid of the song for tidings of her absent lover." (Kenneth Macleod, The Road to the Isles).

Thou speckled little beauteous troutling,
    Where is the lover of my love?
Is he beyond the boisterous waves,
    Holding combat with heroes?

Thou speckled little beauteous troutling,
    Where is the lover of my mind?
Is he out on the gloomy mountain
    Along with the "Gruagach" of the cairn?

Thou speckled little beauteous troutling,
    Where is the lover of my heart?
Is he in the Isle of Youth,
    Along with Osgar, Connlaoch and Fraoch?

Thou speckled little beauteous troutling,
    Where is the lover of my breast?
Is he in Alba or in Erin,
    Or behind the sun asleep?

Thou speckled little beauteous troutling,
    Is the Son of the Virgin with my love?
And may I my sorrow leave
    In the River that fails not for aye?

Young John son of MacNeil

I am the poor woman
Who has been harried,

Ho hi o hu o.

It is not my cattle
Or my horses,
Or that my corn-stacks
Have been scattered;
It is not that my corn-yard
Has gone up in flames,
Or that my mows
Have been plundered;
It is not that my daughter
Has died in childbed,
That drives a woman
To lament a space;

It is not that has harried me,
But that my courtier
Is in prison in Glasgow,
And that they are threatening
To send him to England,
Or to Edinburgh
Of the hundred fashions.
Were a ransom accepted
For my child,
The cattle would not be

Adown the glens;
Horses would not be
Carrying seaweed;
There would be no white
Sheep on the hills.
Goodly son of MacNeil
Once of the Castle,
It is my hand that
Used to bathe thee,
It is my knee that
Used to nurse thee,
It is my breast that
Used to swell thee.
Goodly son of MacNeil
From the tower and the Castle,
Thou didst kill the colonel,
Thou didst wound the captain;
Thou didst bring thine own
Force home with thee,
The host with brown hair
And curling locks;
Thou didst leave the Lowlanders
Dead without life,
The host with polls
Red and bristly.
I am tortured
And tormented,
In my mansion,
In my storehouse;

My sleeping-chamber,
My bedroom:
Though woe is me for that,
It is not what has harried me!

Little sister, my love

Little sister, my love
Art thou asleep?

The brother of ours
Who was in Ireland,

The brother of ours
Who was in Ireland,

Yesterday early they had
Upon the staves.

Yesterday early they had
Upon the staves.

I was beside them
And the rest not seeing me,

Awhile on the ground I was,
Awhile on horseback,

And awhile from their sight
In a green veil folded.

I shall give thee a sign
Of thy dream:

The great byre that
Holds the cattle,

It will be tomorrow
In red flames;

And that little child
Thou hast in thine arms,

Thou wilt find him dead
At the edge of thy bed.

Take that home with thee
As thou hast heard it.

The brother of ours
Who was in Ireland,

Yesterday they had him
Upon the staves.

It was no crew of landsmen

It was no crew of landsmen
Crossed the ferry on Wednesday:
'Tis tidings of disaster if you live not.

What has kept you so long from me
Is the high sea and the sudden wind catching you,
So that you could not at once give her sail.

'Tis a profitless journey
That took the noble man away,
To take our one son from me and from Donald.

My son and my three brothers are gone,
And the one son of my mother's sister,
And, sorest tale that will come or has come, my
    husband.

What has set me to draw ashes
And to take a spell at digging
Is that the men are away with no word of their living.

I am left without fun or merriment
Sitting on the floor of the glen;
My eyes are wet, oft are tears on them.